DELUDED

PAYAL SEHGAL

Copyright © 2025 by **Payal Sehgal**

All rights reserved. No portion of this book may be reproduced in any form without written permission from the publisher or author, except as permitted by Australian Copyright Council (ACC).

It is sold with the understanding that neither the author nor the publisher is engaged in rendering legal, investment, accounting or other professional services. Neither the publisher nor the author shall be liable for any loss of profit or any other commercial damages, including but not limited to special, incidental, consequential, personal, or other damages. For queries visit:

www.payalsehgal.com

ISBN: 978-1-923679-01-6 (paperback)
ISBN: 978-1-923679-00-9 (ebook)

For Rohin, Mihir, and Ishir
Who give me strength and remind me
That every moment of life is precious and worth living for

CONTENTS

Deluded 1

The Clean Slate II 3

The Machine 6

The Hotel 8

The CafÉ 9

The Veil 11

Help 12

The invisible one 13

The One again 14

The Sin 15

Silenced 16

The Laws 17

I am just a chronicler 19

Not when it comes to me 20

It can know 22

Brave 23

Anxiety 24

Psykosis 26

A Lament 28

Love 29

Hope 30

The Now 31

Sadness 32

Hope II 33

The return 34

A Poem 36

Spring	37
No reply	38
Psychosis	39
The Apartment	41
Where they hide	43
Where are they	45
Worries	47
Inspiration	49
Medical History	51
Who am I	52
The Mother	54
Anxiousness	56
To listen or not	58
Peace	61
Death	63
Don't interfere	65
Tears	67
Drained	69
Depression	71
I dream	74
Mine or His	77
Go back where you came from	80
Anger	81
Anger II	83
Mind readers	85
The rhyme	86
Diwali	87

An Acknowledgement	88
Whereabouts unknown	90
Covid	92
The Second Coming	95
A Parody	97
As Time moves on	100
Thoughts	101
Not in my name	104
Sorry	107
About the Author	110

ACKNOWLEDGMENTS

I am an artist and writer who lives in Canberra. I began writing these poems in my journal this year, while existing as if in detention, as my three sons were taken away by their father and his family in 2017. This happened after I was labelled with Schizophrenia and all three of my sons had been bruised.

We are being detained by those who don't believe in Human Rights and between 2018 and 2025, I experienced homelessness and isolation.

My sons have not returned to me as yet but we are in the same city, and, together we are trying to rebuild a life filled with hope and small moments of happiness. Our recovery is slow — there is still too much sadness and anger hiding behind the smiles that others see when we speak to them.

I write when I feel low, angry, sad, or hopeful. My journal has become my constant companion — a space that listens when people can't, or won't. I have reached out to politicians for help, but my pleas have gone unheard. Yet I remain hopeful that someday, someone will listen — not just for me, but for all those whose voices have been silenced.

When you are alone, it helps to know that you are not the only one living with adversity. That thought has guided me to support others — those who are homeless and those living with cancer — as my eldest son also battles a tumour. His brothers and he have given in to their father's desire to live with him as he grows angry and hurts them when I ask to see them. I wonder how many children in the world experience such separation — is it only here in Australia, or everywhere?

I studied poetry in school and naturally gravitated toward telling my story through verse and prose. I now love the free-flowing form of poetry — it mirrors thought as it comes, unfiltered and alive. When I feel empty, I find solace in the company of poets of yore, whose timeless words remind me that poetry can turn even pain into beauty.

I would like to thank Aussie Book Publishers for all of their help and support.

DELUDED

I should never have left his side, they say,

My biggest regret is that I did

And tried to hide my thoughts from him.

I should never have

For he took offence and not rightfully so,

But he did take offence to the fact that I had stopped being

His, completely and solely;

So who did it hurt but our children,

Who got punished, but our children,

He had no right to hurt them but he did;

Truth will out and he will repent,

Who will make him is something

That is open to inspection;

Will it help to know or not,

Will it help to show or not,

Will they cry or will they not,

Is debatable not even;

It will help to have this tale turned out to dry,

And it will help to have his actions turned to nought,

So everyone can tell whether he is bad or not,

Is debatable not even;

For his actions need to be judged,

And my children need to be returned to me;

I write here knowing fully well that no one may read

These thoughts of mine,

Or maybe I know that someone will soon

And I hope not in vain

And the pain will end soon and that my heart will not show so much

Disdain…and soon.

THE CLEAN SLATE II

It's gone they say, the capacity to write,

I know but won't say so

Not so much that they know that I know.

I wonder why I don't want them to know,

Especially when I have said it all,

To the police even;

However, he makes them cry,

And then promise that they will not let anyone know

That he has been cruel to them;

They cry and then they smile when I ask

Them and I know that they are afraid

But won't say anything against him;

What should I do, I am really tired:

He sends them away on holidays,

Takes them to movies,

He spends money like there is no tomorrow,

And children like it so much

That they get pleased but it is like a disease;

I know not what I should write,

I know though that it is depressing to sometimes,

And the pain in the pit gets stronger and stronger,

And that which is there

Will not diminish or not linger;

I see them sometimes

And not too often anymore;

I wonder how many other mothers this happens to,

And how many live without their children,

Who grow up in the custody of villains;

Is it only in Australia that this happens

Or is it all over the world now

Is it only to a certain cultural background

Or is it across cultural boundaries;

For the world is a fairer place now they say,

And what used to happen to one, and I mean Slavery,

Could not happen to another and this easily,

Because of all the laws which were put into place in 1945

Post World War II or was it just history?

THE MACHINE

I went rowing yesterday,

In the bright light of the day,

Not in the waters but indoor rowing,

They said to me when I asked them.

We wheeled them out onto the deck

Where the wading ducks could be seen,

And the ducklings ran in after them;

I was a bit nervous when I went in,

As I had never done something like this before,

And so it was good to meet other participants there,

Who were not from folklore;

Those who knew what it meant

And were there for the whole show;

One had suffered a serious injury,

And his wheelchair could tell all

Where he had not had the will to go;

The instructor started to count,

And we all followed suit;

And what I had been worried about

Went away in a jiffy

As the music started to roar;

It was nice to be rowing

Next to the watery shore;

But what I did not know

Was that I would love it so,

I had wanted to that is why I had gone there

In the first place,

And will do so next week too;

And so I smiled at the man in the wheelchair,

"You can walk again

If you will yourself to."

THE HOTEL

You tread on my dreams

And I know not how to hurt thou;

You think and think o woman from the hotel chain

One will not let you go in vain.

You have hurt my children and I so much

That I will hurt you much

And they will help me once they are older;

They will know you coz I have uttered thy name to them and they

Are colder than they were three years ago;

So be careful coz I have gone cold too and will know how to hurt

again…

Let the vein know that it is not going to go in vain.

THE CAFÉ

I know not how to thank here

As it is also a place where they know me;

Know of my griefs,

But know him more;

He who has taken my sons away from me,

And now has eloped with Time in his cap

To a far away land that I used to call home.

It is not so anymore,

As it is this land which is my children's now,

And it is their laughter,

And their snippety snippets,

That I long for and live for;

I don't know how to thank here,

Coz they know me here,

But also can't know me,

As the King's colony will not let them know me, they say;

I who only started to know 10 years ago

That everyone knows more than me,

Know not how to ask for help

From those who were brought in

By their partners only?

THE VEIL

I scream in pain,

Why don't they know that I know when they think;

They know that my sons are being abused,

But they won't help me

Just because I am a non-white.

I can't see my own people

Without their constant gaze upon my neck;

Why don't they see

That by watching me nonstop,

They are opening doors

For the rest of the world to look into;

I am being detained here by them,

And the whole world will see what is happening;

This is Schizophrenia, I ask you

A thinly veiled attempt

To keep a woman away from the rest of society.

HELP

As I walked up to them,

I knew that they were someone who I needed to talk to;

And of course one of them I did know,

And it was nice to connect,

And meet all those others who help those who don't have a home.

All benefactors, in their own way,

All helping those who are there,

I asked for help too,

And it was given;

I am grateful and thankful,

And hope to meet them again;

And HelpingACT, I have told my sons about you too;

Let's hope that you will be able to bring them home somehow,

Coz it is really difficult to be a woman who has to live without a home

And know that tomorrow is there for #metoo.

THE INVISIBLE ONE

I know thy Voice,

I know all of thy traits

How dare you think that you will be fine

O petty one;

You have messed with my life

You have taken my children away from me.

I will see to it that you end up smelling a Courtroom;

And then you will see whether it was fine to abuse and then make

Money or not;

Stop thinking and you will be fine

I have been hinting for a while;

Why are you so slow

That your mind does not know

That it will get emptied

Into the vast emptiness that they call life…and soon.

THE ONE AGAIN

Don't say Sorry in vain,

You give me a headache when you do;

And all this because I know that you are not Sorry

But just happy that I am still in this shed.

Just wait for a while

And then you will see,

That those who get bullied

Do come out of their pain as the Gods really send help their way;

And it has come in a way

From my family overseas,

Who will not hurt me

But have helped as they know that by doing so

Thy corrupt ways will really hurt for good now or is it I who knows it so;

Just you wait, just for a while.

THE SIN

One knows not what one doth know,

What one knows one does not know;

Two ways of saying the same things,

What should I do I am fine too.

They just don't understand

That by bullying me they are interfering with God's people,

He knows and has stopped in a way but they won't;

It says in the Magical world

That one must not bully in this space;

Coz what goes around comes around,

And those who hurt others or think of hurting them

Are sinning and will not know love from God or their Demon;

So sin not coz lives are at stake here,

And what one knows not,

One can know and not hurt at will.

SILENCED

I wonder how she can silence

Women who are being abused by their men,

She knows that I can't live alone,

And must cry when I am in my home all alone.

She who cares about feminism so,

Knows DV, even helps those

Who are not as lucky as her;

It is she who asked me out!

She singled me out then,

And I went quiet

As I listened to her talk

About the past.

THE LAWS

The Middle Ages, that is where we all are still,

The rest of the world has moved on,

But Australia is still trapped in the whirlpool.

Let go, I say as I swirl in the deep waters,

Nay we won't we are the Nazis

Who like to abuse colored migrants now,

As the Indigenous have a right to life in some parts of the country,

For their people are allowed to support them now;

Indians must die though, we say,

As they don't have their country's laws here anymore;

They let go of their Citizenship,

And their husbands who wanted to annihilate them but couldn't

So we are here to do their bidding instead;

And we will continue to hurt you

As the Assembly says no when you go to it;

But Coercive Control will become a crime

In ACT Public Law one day soon!

I AM JUST A CHRONICLER

Can I ask you something,

"Do you hear Voices in your head,"

That is a constant refrain,

So I say to them that I don't,

I am just a Reiki Healer and believe in Intuition.

It guides me and helps me to believe myself,

And in any case all streams prove that

It is possible to follow your dreams without

Someone telling you otherwise;

And then the thought comes in

That he lies but it is I who has been called a liar

By the Clinic.

NOT WHEN IT COMES TO ME

Imagine if it had happened to you,

I once said to the psychiatrist;

She, in turn, asked me to talk to DVCS,

Which has finally acknowledged DV for me,

But still asks my children to come forward.

The Tribunal has acknowledged it too,

But will not know me now,

Past the note that says I do not need a PTO;

A seizure hurts one, the other two call 000,

I am glad there were no outages when they had to;

That is what the thought thinks—

It is not a sin to think that;

O, those who do not pray,

When will you know

That ours is a multicultural city;

The Chief says so, too,

But not when it comes to me.

IT CAN KNOW

Read yesterday in the Essential Jung

That he used to maintain,

That even those who are not lovers can know the same things,

As it is the Occult or Clairvoyance

That makes Psychiatrists think.

My eyes well up

When I write this,

A little like how I feel every morning…

I wonder and know

That my three also feel the same sometimes and wonder

Why those who know me

Can't know that they are really alone,

And not that well without their mother.

BRAVE

I write now as I can write no more,

That those who sowed the seeds of hope in me

Have moved on.

But they are still here,

And I just have to be brave and reach out and ask for help,

And the heavens will open up and shower their blessings upon me;

My sons have all grown up,

And I cry not in vain

When I think of the past that was here but was taken away

By a few men and women's hate.

ANXIETY

I know not what the present holds,

I know not what the future holds either;

All I know for sure is that the past that has been

Has been erasing itself hatefully.

And what can be undone is history

And what can be said and redone is not really the story;

Can I be that good, I do not know

Coz my anxiety doth help not,

All it does is hurt when it should not;

Does it hurt me or another,

I know not for sure;

I really need to live through each moment

To know whether I should have known or not known;

How old am I,

I feel like 32 or 33

When in IRL,

I am fifty three.

PSYKOSIS

I got here and started to know him really well in 2015;

It's called Psychosis

As it leads to a lot of fear,

Fear of the unknown and fear of the real.

A stepping across boundaries,

A kneeling into the pews,

A submission of guilt or not

But a submission of another reality;

I wish that I had been allowed to know this when I was younger,

But I was never allowed to fall in love, not like she was,

Although I was;

I did give myself the chance,

But father did not really know;

And what was real was turned into the surreal

And mother was the only one who knew

But she also thought that it was wrong,

And it probably was;

It's called abuse now

But then I gave it a name that rhymes with dove;

Did not know then, however,

That people, when they see the woman alone,

Call it Psychosis

Greek for Psykosis - falling in love.

A LAMENT

663 Words later and I still do not know

That no one will know my story

Even though everyone knows.

Our tears have gone but the sadness is still there,

Hiding behind the smiling faces

Glad that we all are still here;

Will we live together, we know not,

Will we be able to share our lives again, we know not;

It says that yes it will happen,

But God what is here today was not there yesterday

And that which was here yesterday is gone today or not.

LOVE

I write poetry now when I used to write prose before,

It is fine to do so, I hear you say,

But I do not know why it is here but not within my grasp,

The word that was here yesterday

Has gone today but almost not.

I know thy love coz I know thy pain,

Do you know mine though,

That I live without hate?

Will you come back,

Will it help to have you back,

I do not know;

Will I lose them once again,

Or will thy love show?

HOPE

You don't need to know me

Others will;

And some of them will say to you

That you should have known me but I will say that it's fine

Not everyone needs to know my story.

So fret not,

Don't shed tears of sorrow,

Coz what you think is dead is still there for the morrow.

THE NOW

I know my own story so well

That I forget to tell others what it is;

And they wonder whether I am fine

As what is not really there in the lime will light really soon.

But first my sons and I need to help others

Or do we need to help ourselves first;

Do we forgive each other and know that it is fine to erase the memories

Of the past here;

Coz what was anxiety then is the past now,

What was anger then is sadness now;

And what is real is the present,

And what must be worked on

Is this that we call real.

SADNESS

I have a catch in my throat today

It is not too big but just a sadness inside me that is being contained within.

I wrote to them today but I did not say that I had been labelled Mentally Ill;

Will they know me now or will they shake their heads and delete me from their history?

HOPE II

I write and write

And everyone sends me their good wishes,

I know that it is all real

As I sit here and write in this journal.

What is it that I need to know,

It is all here:

Good things are happening

And good people are coming my way

Just a matter of time

Before they come back

And know my ways.

THE RETURN

It's like the creative energy's gone for a while;

It was there but now it is not,

What should I do but write as they used to say,

The lecturers i.e.

Coz it is not that my mind has dried up

But it is that I don't have anything to say over here.

I believe in good but they don't,

I believe in being kind but they don't,

I believe that by letting go of hate

One heals oneself;

But they don't,

And they listen and interfere with my life,

The blessings don't come my way anymore,

But they do;

I know that I write here

Knowing that it will come back to me,

And the writer's block that comes in the way

Will unblock itself and unfold,

And the wrapping will unwrap itself

And what was once will not be again;

But it could come in another way.

A POEM

This has become a journal of poems

Which is a great way

To let go of one's anxieties.

So this is what I do

When I can't write stories:

The poems flow into my heart

And then my mind

And what I used to see

Cannot be now seen,

And what comes to me

Is a little poem

That I could have written

When they were babies.

SPRING

It is spring

And summer's just round the corner;

The weather is turning warmer,

And the wind is picking up.

Some wonder why this happens…

It does so that the air can get clean again,

And those of us who could not breathe too well

The cold air

Can walk once more

With spring in our steps,

And, again.

NO REPLY

I wonder why I feel so low

When the day was not that bad:

I found a cardigan, one that I had been looking for for a while,

Even saw an apartment I liked,

Met a lady who understood me totally,

Wrote to a lawyer who knows how to help those who need support,

those like me.

But there has been no reply

And I wonder why,

Is it that he could have forgotten me

Or is it that everyone is just plain busy?

I should write to her again

And ask for more intros or not,

Or maybe I will wait for a while, just tonight,

Give it one more day

And that which was not returned may come my way.

PSYCHOSIS

It should be compulsory for all to study poetry

When they are in school -

Up until year 10 at least.

The pain of knowing or is it the pleasure

That what is yours can be another's too,

Only in a slightly different form;

And the multicultural world that we live in

Was formed where else but in the dormitory?

What of those of us who did not stay in boarding

But were day scholars,

All really good at adapting

Not just the teacher's refrain

But also that of the rest of the class,

Which lags behind but not in vain;

For those of us who come late or last

Do get there eventually,

And I who was always first in class

Was embarrassed that I got here this late -

At the age of 43;

This they call Psychosis,

An interesting phenomenon we thought yesterday,

But what is more difficult to fathom

Is that Schizophrenia or Delusional disorder is the next step of

Psychosis,

And that Psychiatrists just label people

For ex-husbands and ex-mother-in-laws

Just so that they can make it difficult for those of us who are sane;

It really hurts children

Who don't know how to support themselves

When they find themselves totally alone,

Totally alone and broken, and, well-meaning people

Who don't know the sane from insane hurt them just the same.

THE APARTMENT

Am looking at properties to buy,

And went to see two

With one before we dropped the other one off

At Deakin oval;

Something that brought back

Difficult memories of time past.

The suburb of Franklin is easy to navigate,

But the apartments we saw

Were not what I expected them to be;

There is another one

Have asked to view that,

As we missed the morning inspection;

We had lunch in Dickson,

And I noticed another apartment

Open for inspection,

So I booked an Uber

And rushed to view it;

It was lovely and inviting

Right opposite City Centre,

And have asked her

If I can see it again with my sons;

She said she will let me know by tonight

And then I will know

Whether it is the one.

WHERE THEY HIDE

It was difficult to rent

As my rental history was tarnished;

But that was back in 2018

And he has let go of me

But his dogs haven't,

They still bark.

And they still think

That I will not be successful

In my bid to buy a place;

It will happen in good time, I am sure,

But patience runs thin

As those who know me wonder

Why a woman like me

Is having such a difficult time

Finding peace;

But the Anti migration rally

Has left its mark

On those who like to bully migrants

And they attack from behind still;

Just a matter of time though

Before the international police comes in,

Not everyone is anti-Republic here

And they may think that they will win,

But really the men and women should know better and go quiet

As Cassius Turvey's mother is still around,

Listening to the pleas

Of those whose sons

Have been bruised badly,

And all by these whiffers and sneaky people

Who like to pretend

That they are multicultural now.

WHERE ARE THEY

Voices:

Depression

Psychosis

Schizophrenia and now

Delusional Disorder.

Am I really in love

With someone from a higher caste or status,

Sarcasm intended!

But I know from previous experience

(And I am 53 now)

That if I care about them

Then they do too;

She said to me the other day

That of course you are Mentally Ill, i.e. Depressed,

The things that you have been through,

And I hadn't even told her my whole story;

How astute are some people in this city

We need more like them;

And, actually,

She doesn't live in this city

But in NSW;

All good people live in that State

And there is a dearth of good ones

In this city.

WORRIES

So I was writing about Voices:

He used to use them to depress me

And make me alone.

I used to worry a lot

When I would be home alone

And this I have been doing since my childhood,

But not like I would have to

After I had had my children,

Post-natal Depression it is called;

A palmist once said to me,

"You think too much,"

He meant that I worry too much;

I do,

But it helps to know

That there are others who worry so much

That they threaten to hurt me

And take my sons away from me;

It gives me a strange sort of satisfaction

As my sons love me so much

That they keep coming back to me,

And I am really sure

That they will never let go of me;

Even the one who threatened me yesterday

That he would start a lawsuit against me,

Even he will not let go

And will come back to me,

Eventually.

INSPIRATION

Inspiration, you have run dry again,

I think of thee and I write over here;

Will you come back to me

And make me write as you do sometimes?

I really need to write a story

But I do think that I will have to move

Into a finer place

For me to do so;

Just a few more weeks

And it will happen,

Why can't I be patient till then?

But I have this catch in my throat

And it hurts too much

As my sons are away from me still,

And he who knows thinks of me

But is letting me make it easier for myself still:

Find your way in life, like a mentor he says,

Do I need a mentor or a friend or a lover

Someone who will bring them back to me;

Time has a habit of moving on though

And they cry a bit and ask him why

He can't come now,

To which he replies,

I have thought of coming in February

And will only come then;

O thought, why can't you come sooner,

I can buy a property but not really bring them back

As they have made a silent promise

To their father and his - that they won't let anyone know

How he detains them or even that he does;

Never ever have I felt this alone or sad

That I am a woman.

MEDICAL HISTORY

I just learnt that today is International Menopause Day –

18th of October;

Peri started for me in March this year

And has been a welcome addition to my life.

Although the antipsychotics that I am being forced to take,

And those that tell me to go to sleep at 9:15 PM

Just so that I cannot have a social life anymore,

Are really interfering with their Voices

And their thinking patterns and their medication;

And it was nice to hear

That the Psychiatrist wants me

To go to my GP now;

I will know for sure next week

What they are thinking

But one said today that I now have a right

To go to a practitioner of my choice!

WHO AM I

What will I do till then?

I am here but not really there.

I walk and do things everyday

And my life seems to have a meaning,

But only when they are with me

Do I feel like I have a purpose still;

It's sad that it has come to this

And I don't know why I am like this now;

Maybe it's because I am older now,

Maybe it's because I know too

That I can't be a mother anymore,

As they don't need me like they used to,

Then who am I?

Why am I alive still?

Is it for all those other women

Who lose their children to their ex-partners?

For all those women

That is what my life is for;

Like she said the other day

Before receiving the Award

For Australian of the Year;

I am here for them only;

For my sons too, of course

But that is even though

I feel sad

That they don't need me

Like they used to.

THE MOTHER

And also as I don't want them to know

The loss that I knew

When she passed away at a young age.

Too soon her passing away was

And who did it help

But those who live for the moment only;

Not even her

Even though she had wanted to die;

She lived with me for 5 years after that,

Not here,

Nor really there either;

A loss for all to bear,

But a loss

That only those who are there can know;

And know,

And be sad,

And shed a tear,

When the loved one does not show;

Why did she go away so soon,

I still ask even though I know

That there were forces

That did not want her to live;

Swept in the desire to live or kill as they were,

These same forces

Would want me to die too;

But I live for my sons

As I don't want them to know yet

What I knew

When I was 36.

ANXIOUSNESS

I listen to you tube as I write here,

It's a nice song

And it brings back memories of her

And of life back in India.

I went back this year

After 11 years of not having gone,

I went coz they helped me;

I really did not want to go back for the wedding

As they are too real,

And too happy

And I would not have been able to hide

The sadness within me;

They would not have come with me

So I said no;

Two said, yes, this year

But my brother was alone

So it was I who said, no, this time,

And went back on my own;

Get your visas and come soon,

I advised them

Before joining the queue of eager travelers;

The regret stays though

As my grand-aunt did not really know me;

It was different when I went back with one of them,

Only my sister was anxious now

But she had been anxious earlier too.

TO LISTEN OR NOT

I don't know if I can pretend or wait till next year

To know someone who does not want to know me now.

Is it wrong they ask to not listen to your own thought?

Nay, I hear it say, it is not my thought,

It is yours and I don't know why I should listen to you now

When you did not to me then;

I did not know that you wanted me to listen to you!

I did not know that you wanted me to meet you

And get to know you;

I don't think much of myself

When it comes to those who think

I am someone who they should meet;

I am feeling a bit low today

And it is because my eldest and I had a disagreement yesterday

And he has said, yet again,

That he won't meet me for another two months or so;

This even though his father is not here

But in India,

At least the younger two are there

And I do have a mission at hand -

I have to buy a house

And maybe find work too;

It will pass this time too

But he hurts himself now

And knowingly, too knowingly;

Be complacent - Not!

I had said to all three yesterday

But that is exactly what they are now;

And so when I said

That they could subpoena him,

One said,

That we will ask him to take our side instead!

They want you here,

Why can't you come for a little while

Then go back where you came from,

It will be fine

I will not say anything, I promise,

Or will I?

I will not be sitting with all three for a while;

Why do I tell them everything,

They just don't understand

That I worry because I care.

PEACE

I can think but you can't,

You are just a figment;

I know you,

You have a name

And you have proven

That you are real.

But you can't think with me,

It hurts too much and I am alone here;

They bully like dogs now,

They see me as colored

And I don't have a right

To life in theirs,

So don't think coz you are too far away;

I am not being silly today

Just don't know what to do

As I swore on the streets today,

Maybe just under my breath,

Or maybe not under my breath;

What would she have thought of me,

Her favourite daughter, I used to think.

What will she think of me;

Please thoughts,

Don't be so cruel,

I am a real person

And people judge here;

We can't be friends anymore

But at least let's not be enemies.

Tell thy friends that,

Let others know

That I come in peace

Even when it looks like I don't…

DEATH

It's a sad day

And I type here,

Thinking whether I want to

Coz all I am doing

Is typing my sadness

Here on this blank page.

It hurts

Or it does not,

I know not anymore…

Ok, stop then, the thought says

But I keep typing

Like I can hear no more;

Ok, Stop; Stop;

It makes not any sense your thought

Or maybe it does,

But I know not how I will live,

But I know too that I have to;

Aren't you all lucky

That I live

For my sons three,

Imagine what a death

Could do to you all;

Although Suicide

I don't believe in,

Someone would have to come

And kill me,

And there is no one here

In this city who would do that

To me.

DON'T INTERFERE

I write knowing

That no one knows why I do;

They think that I follow them

When in reality

It is they who do my bidding.

I think and they divine,

They just do not know

That in the meditator's world,

It is wrong to interfere

With another's thoughts;

J.K Rowling wrote in Harry Potter

That those who interfere with magic

Will really get punished one day!

That day is nigh

I have been told…

It makes me a little slow

When he gets upset,

But it is fine,

Coz he knows here that he cares about me,

And, I about him;

My younger two do too

They do divine too;

We know that the end is nigh

And that which seems like eternity will be over

In a mere snap of the fingers;

And it will be soon when we will live together again,

His tyranny will end soon

As Justice doth come to those who wait eagerly;

And know that that which is gone

Is still here;

Life is short but love is real

Between a Mother and her sons.

TEARS

I cry silent tears,

I don't know why or maybe I do,

I know not why I shed these tears

But they are there morning and night now.

I have to be full of hope

As I can't let go of its side now

Coz they are thinking, I know,

Even those who have hurt me

And those who have hurt themselves more,

Are thinking why they are punishing

Three young men who take the punishment silently;

Don't they know

That they can come over

And ask for help from me,

Or do they,

They do meet me as often as they can,

At least two do;

The third likes to punish himself,

He was always like that–

Stubborn and defiant;

He used to not listen to me

When I would tell him to:

Don't become your father's follower,

Coz it will hurt you one day,

I used to say.

DRAINED

I woke up to thoughts

Of his wife and him;

He has a life there,

I don't have one here or maybe I do.

I just need to not expect help

From those who have hurt themselves,

No one is perfect, I say, I least of all of them;

Not that I have done anything

But I have been supporting my sons,

Who I know have been punished

By that man who taped me;

Is it a sin then

To say that you don't know for sure,

Is it a sin then

To say that I don't know

Whether they cry there or not,

Is it a sin then to see it all

And then tell the world what you saw;

I am a blind woman

Or visually impaired,

I do not have laser vision

Like I know my ex does

With his vast connections in the capitalist world;

I am in a mafia movie,

And it would have been nice

Had he come to get me,

Like the hero does at the end;

But it is not the end as yet

And no one is dying,

Much as I wrote that we all were:

Drained,

Would have been a better word.

DEPRESSION

Devoid of all thought

And dependents now,

That is who we are.

I want to pull myself

Out of this Depression

And I know that I will,

But will my sons, especially my eldest?

It's hurting him,

And he has been scared no end

By none other than the man

Who carries a gun within his head:

It pulsates when he is angry,

And only the one who is near him

Can see it getting madder and madder,

And those who are not near him

Cannot know what anger means,

As he shows it not

To anyone but the one who is near him;

(And those who don't know poems

Really don't know how to go quiet

In the presence of those who do know them;

Who are they,

Why can't they know

That they have been let off the hook but not that much

If they can't go quiet!)

I was threatened by a Vice Chancellor in 2019,

That I should not talk about my project on DV but I will now,

As I am not that scared anymore;

Intuition guides me

And I have said it to nurses,

And they all agree,

It is not Voices that I hear

As they are really confusing

And do not let you think for yourself,

It is called Depression that state

And my three are really depressed too;

They just absorb everything around them,

And this city is full of dark people

Who are fair looking,

But are not when you talk to them;

There are too many of them

In their father's social circle,

And they meet them often

As they are the only ones they are allowed to meet;

Depression is everywhere

But Intuition will guide you out of its depths,

If you let it and listen

To its silent sounds;

Go quiet and don't think for a while

But meditate,

And let your mind

Take control of all sound.

I DREAM

Sitting in the Seoul Sistaz,

I wonder why I am feeling so low,

It's not that I did not know,

He hath said no;

But the heart still entertains

A belief that time will still know.

And now with that news still in the news

I wonder whether he will be strong enough to know,

Or will he stay quiet like he has been,

I do hope in my heart of hearts that he won't;

What hurts though

Is that they will not have the strength to fight,

A night like yesterday;

Uneventful as it was,

I woke up feeling low;

He was there

And so were they, all three of them.

They know men who like guns,

I do too,

But I don't like it

When they are used to hurt innocents;

I was married to one

Once upon a time;

Did not know it then

That he was fine with anger

And punishment meted out

To those undeserving of it;

And now my heart hurts,

Coz I know one who likes to do the same:

Am I a masochist?

I have known for a while;

My sons too are like me

Punishing themselves still

After the light has gone;

The sounds may have gone too,

But the memories remain;

And he will bring them back

Unless they change before he comes back -

The villain who could not steal my heart,

And so he killed me,

Murdered my instincts,

Annihilated my dreams;

But one dream he cannot take away:

And that

Is that their love for me

Still remains.

MINE OR HIS

I still feel low and empty,

The day is hot but not sultry;

All seems quiet,

The music plays on low;

The café is empty,

And I remain alone.

The mood is hurried,

But the steps are slow;

The heart does not race,

But the mind does;

The thing to know

Is that no one can know,

But everyone does;

I talk and they go quiet,

I stay hushed

And they know all still;

Probably better to not tell then

As what the heart knows

Is another's secret:

A killer's dream,

That is what the secret is;

A Mental Illness it is called

But the time is nigh

When the Mentally Ill shall rejoice;

And those who race you out of it

Would like to know,

But don't want to know,

That their end is nigh too;

Who are they, I ask you

Splashed all over the news as they are;

The Police are tired of them,

As they race through

The city of Melbourne;

When will ours know that it is wrong to bully women -

All Mothers who know not anything

But their children's love,

A love as pure as the snow

That floats down from the skies above;

Not as harsh as the sun here in this city,

That I have been calling home since the 1990s,

But as soft as the flakes that one sees here once in a while,

Not that I want to without them;

Life, it seems, has gone dull for a while,

And what was once hopeful and full of desire,

Lies squashed and pale,

Like the ale in the window out yonder;

A tale for all to hear and wonder.

Which one though, I ask you

Mine or his?

GO BACK WHERE YOU CAME FROM

They live in sewers,

But pretend to be human;

They shriek nonstop,

Like only the vermin can.

They will come for them the cleaners

And then they will know;

Killing a woman's dreams,

And not just the woman's

But the children's too;

All hate colored migrants

NO, they hate themselves

And wish that they hadn't been born;

They should really go back

Where they came from.

ANGER

I have to have every single one of you punished

And I take the oath on the Day of Diwali;

You are really hurting Indians too much,

I will know not but others in India will really know

What you are doing to my sons and I on this day of Diwali;

Even my sons don't know it,

Born as they were over here.

Sorry, sorry, will not be enough,

It will be money that you will lose

And so much of it that you will not be able to recover

From the loss,

All of you, especially the Legislative Assembly that started it

And the hotel that it began in;

The rioters will know too,

The witches all of you as you float higher and higher,

You will get disabled too like I have been;

And that man who has started this torture will hurt in his own way,

He is a killer guys, when you just kill dreams;

Had you listened to me and gone quiet,

I would not have had to take an oath that you will hurt

And get punished;

A fanatic I am too not just you,

Which is funny as I am half catholic too!

So remember that your hate will not go in vain,

As I am here to not take the pain for too long;

Embarrassed me no end you and your Anglo-Saxon men,

O you dirty woman, it is not long before they come and get you so

don't shout!

ANGER II

I don't know what to write

But I do know that what I have to say

Will be listened to by those who know human rights.

There is so much racism in the city now

Or is it classicism;

He can just make me homeless

And his people can evict me from their hotels,

And poor Mental Health Workers call this a Mental Illness!

All of this was made illegal in the Republic of India in 1947;

We just need a Republic here

As the Colony is really hurting those

Who believe in Equality for all peoples, whether rich or poor.

Australia says that it is a Socialist State,

But it is just where Capitalism reigns;

I am fine coz I have the money to support myself now,
But those who are poor don't have the same luxury;

I have given myself one year,
Rather two more months
Before it gets better for us:
By the end of the year, or early next year.

MIND READERS

I know not what to write

But I will write some more.

So they read my mind,

And I know not how to tell them to not do so;

I will have to write about the magical world then,

But first I will have to get a place to call my own;

I go to the city so often

That it could be fine to make an offer there;

But what do I do about my sons

They are here and need a home with their mother,

Their mater still.

THE RHYME

It is not without peace;

It is hopeful,

But it is not so.

It comes and it goes,

It shows,

But it does not show;

It returns

And it starts into the future,

It is something

That all will know in their own good time;

What am I,

I do not know myself,

But I think

That I begin with T

And rhyme with chime.

DIWALI

I think that I am going mad,

Or is it sad.

I do not know

Whether they will come today or not,

Although they have promised to do so;

I go to the temple alone

And I hope that they will stay,

Even though one has said that he won't

As he has a prior engagement;

Diwali comes once every year only,

But they all have grown up

Without me so, that they won't know my ways anymore,

Much as I will…

AN ACKNOWLEDGEMENT

Not in the country,

Or the world,

That day will come soon

When Women will have more rights.

We must not falter,

Nor must we stop to take a breath

That makes us think

That we can't do

What those before us

Have done for the woman-kind;

I think not,

Nor do I breathe,

But I wonder why I am still alive

If not to lead;

Lead those who have been abused,

Lead those who have been mistreated,

And Lead those who have been broken

Not by themselves,

But by those whom they trusted;

They are here now,

Those who support a woman like me:

So women thanks heaps

For acknowledging me.

WHEREABOUTS UNKNOWN

The woman has hurt my children and I so much

That I am tired of her shrieks now,

And can ask her to go quiet

And not hurt herself so.

But I don't know where she is,

Even though I know that her real self

Lives in a hotel chain

That I was taken away from

By the Clinic and its workers in 2022;

She smiled and laughed silently

As I was taken away;

But the last laugh will be mine

Coz you do know

How much my sons and I have hurt since then;

And it is my ex-husband's fault

That this has happened,

I do know,

But it is wrong

To support such wrongs.

COVID

So desirous were they of evil

That they hurt no end with their dark magic,

Little did they know

That by doing so they were taking away my thoughts,

And this, as any self-respecting magician would know,

Is a sin in the world of Magic.

But there is a dearth of such magicians in Canberra,

Started to happen when Ken Behrens worked hard

To keep magic to themselves in the time of Covid19;

How much did we lose

When we lost touch with reality

And hurt those who we did not know,

By accepting that it was the flu that was hurting us,

When in reality our own thoughts

Kept us away from helping those

Who were within reach and not too far away from us;

Although the leader also suggested

That it was the best thing to do

And 1.5 came in…

I was forced to stay away from my sons then

As one of them tested positive for Covid:

He was not allowed to go out,

And it used to hurt as I would sit near his place,

And wait to catch a glimpse of him;

I wondered if it was real,

As he was someone who was always strong,

And his immune system too good to be true;

But it was the regulation and had to be observed,

The funny thing, however,

Was that my ex-husband forced all of my sons

To live in the same small apartment

For the days of quarantine;

Had he been good

He would have let my other two come to me

During this time of separation;

It was also during that time that

The PM sent me a letter saying

That he couldn't release my superannuation,

Even though I had written to him that I needed it

As my ex-husband had made me homeless

And time was in suspension;

I really needed a house to stay in,

But the hotel I was staying in just smiled

And said that that must be difficult to take in,

And turned me away after a while.

THE SECOND COMING

And now as I sit here

In this one bedroom place,

Which I want to move out of

As soon as I can get a place,

They shriek and they shout

And they think that no one can hear from yonder,

That the world is full of dark ones

Who look fair in real life but are not,

And we all are left to wonder.

But do we wonder,

Or are there those who tell us to not worry,

As the time is here

When He will come over,

The Messiah,

As it is the Second Coming in Christianity and Islam,

And Kalki's age is here too if you believe it;

The holy Jesuits will know

That what they have done in the name of color

Will change soon;

The Jessicas have begun to shudder

And get asked to leave the shadow ministry,

And their own will hurt them

As they bully and belittle

Those who are of the weaker gender.

A PARODY

I know but don't know why I worry,

When those who are belittling me

Will turn into littler men and women

With their whole families.

Teachers have spoken,

The Shays, the Teghans, The Maureens,

The Xaras, the Heremys and the like

Will not hurt us too much,

As the Tribunal has said

That it is fine to worry about one's children,

Whether colored or not;

I have lost in yours but won in mine,

As my sons and I are still alive,

And we are here to tell our stories;

Mental Health Workers

You may be able to scare my children now,

But me you can only hurt a little

Bit as I know how to get help

And ask for relief

From others who help those like me;

Just a matter of time

As I don't even worry anymore

But just type away, with the sounds of the keys

Jumping to and fro,

Playing a melody for all to hear;

Only I sit alone,

And those who are there cannot know

And only those who are not in the moment can know;

Is this why they say

That the country is not doing well

But instead of blaming the other party it would be nice

Were they to look at their own people;

A glance into the mirror

And they will know

That the country is wasting its time

Playing games of witchcraft and witchery;

And this is called the Mental Health Act,

When all it is

Is a thinly veiled secret

That hurts those who are in minority

But able to help their own quite ably.

AS TIME MOVES ON

How much can I know

I ask myself,

As I think of seeing this and that both.

Will I be able to make it to the show

Or will it run away,

The Time, as I will it to not go -

To not go away with the others,

With those who don't know that I am here for a reason:

I have to bring freedom to the country,

And those who hurt me spiritually

Know not that I know their ways;

Pray to your God if you will but you will know in a little while,

That some countries prosper

Because they believe in all the gods of the world

And don't hurt at will.

THOUGHTS

What should I write here

Sitting beside a cup of tea,

It is empty my mind as I think why

Others say that they don't know when they do.

How many others does it happen to, I will find out:

That was the aim of my project in 2019,

The one that they could not work on with me;

Don't know there,

They will hurt, the thought said,

No, they won't, say I,

Times have changed and it is fine

To not discriminate anymore

That is what they say now;

And the public servants will know

What others have omitted to or ignored,

It's sweet really that all I have to do

Is wait for time to turn its tide;

There are other thoughts

That tell me to wait and be patient;

People rush by on the streets

As the rain comes down slowly but surely,

Persistent and unrelenting;

They bring respite these drops,

Unlike the thoughts that rain continuously,

Have been raining since 2022 now;

It is sad but they don't know that they will be hurting soon,

They must not read the paper

That is why they don't know how the country really works

When it's like this;

He thinks too, I know he does,

Coz he has let go of his anger

And has said that I can work here,

But some in the art community still won't know me;

His Advisor comes to my place

And knows that I don't lie,

They will help but when?

Maybe I expect too much,

When I should just sit and wait

For time to turn its tide;

My ex has gone to India for two months,

And my sons may find the strength

To come and live with me

And things will be fine by and by.

Written from the premises of Seoul Sistaz

NOT IN MY NAME

My mother was one of the best school principals in India,

And I can't be anyone in this country?

What is this place?

How many others does it turn into no one?

Who are these people who are detaining intelligence so?

God will really hurt them

Coz all thoughts come from elsewhere,

The Gods know it well;

We have to be indebted to each other if we must exist as a society,

Don't hurt the Natives and let go of my sons and I

Coz we are tired of this hegemony;

Don't go to the outback

And don't do what you have been doing since 1799

Or whenever yours came here to this country;

Go there,

And help those who look after the land instead

And bring food to the kitchens of us people;

You consume the land

When you hurt the dwellers of the outback;

Don't you know, o city dwellers,

You are hurting no one but yourselves

By tampering with the environment so;

How many Indigenous do you kill everyday,

Did you know that the UN

Is also keeping count and will tell you one day

And then it is your economy that will suffer;

You are hurting someone in your own country

And it is unethical and criminal to do so now;

You also hurt the beings of another country

When you hurt us;

India is a free economy

And I am Indian first

As I look like one

Before I can say that I am Australian;

A first generation Migrant
I am a Republican at heart;
They hurt there and I hurt here;
Don't hurt us Australians so…

SORRY

I detest those who hurt children in anyway;

And you all have been hurting my children

And reaping hate everywhere.

He has gone, the tiller, and, his fate is sealed;

He is an Australian too

And you are hurting him by killing people who are like me;

He used to look after the rivers

Now there is salt everywhere,

Cries of sorry are everywhere

And the worries are there for all to see;

O you Mental Health Worker,

Time will hurt you and it will happen soon;

It has happened already,

Coz your Clinic has almost said sorry to me;

Who am I, but the Economy,

And, your jobs are in jeopardy,

O you lovers of the Man, he is not God but you support him;

It is not allowed over the border but it is in this county?

They know it now,

And it is just a matter of time

Coz they also live here in this land of disdain,

And you may have made it your main source of income,

But it will not be in vain my murder and the murder of my intuition;

It will not be in vain

The killings of my children's innocence;

I pity your children that they have parents like you,

How dare you be allowed to have children

They should be taken away from you.

Like mine were, by you.

To be continued…

ABOUT THE AUTHOR

Payal Sehgal is an artist and writer who lives in Canberra, Australia. She is also a single mother, and much of her work is deeply shaped by lived experience, resilience, and reflection on justice, belonging, and human dignity.

Her writing is concerned with the lived realities of marginalised voices, particularly indigenous communities and migrants in Australia. She reflects on how systems of power, silence, and punishment can impact families— especially women, who even in contemporary society, find themselves separated from their children and live with homelessness.

Through poetry and prose, Payal explores themes of identity, loss, endurance, hope, and survival. Her work seeks not only to tell a personal story, but also to raise questions about equity, compassion, and the kind of society we are shaping for future generations.

www.ingramcontent.com/pod-product-compliance
Lightning Source LLC
Chambersburg PA
CBHW071213070526
44584CB00019B/3017